HOW TO TRANSFORM THINKING, FEELING AND WILLING

Practical exercises for the training of thinking, feeling, willing, imagination, composure, intuition, positivity and wonder

by Jörgen Smit

translated by
Simon Blaxland de Lange

A path leading from the spiritual in human beings to the spiritual in the world

HAWTHORN PRESS

Cover design by Ivon Oates.
Typeset by Jahweh Associates, Stroud.
Printed by Redwood Books, Wiltshire.
Reprint 1998.

Translated from the German, *Freiheit Erüben, Meditationen in der Erkenntnispraxis der Anthroposophie,* by Jörgen Smit, Georg Kühlewind, Rudolf Treichler, Christof Lindenau.

© 1988 Verlag Freies Geistesleben GmbH Stuttgart
English edition copyright © 1989 Hawthorn Press
1 Lansdown Lane, Stroud, Glos. U.K. GL5 1BJ

Cover photo by Nick Hackett.
Cover design by Patrick Roe.
Typeset in Plantin by Jahweh Associates, Stroud.
Printed in Great Britain.

British Library Cataloguing in Publication Data

Smit, Jorgen
How to transform thinking, feeling and willing: practical exercises for the training of thinking, feeling, willing, imagination, composure, intuition, positivity and wonder.
— (Social Ecology Series).
1. Meditation
I. Title II. Series
158'.12

ISBN 1 869 890 17 5

Contents

One should not think 'mystically' about meditation, nor should one think about it in a frivolous way. Meditation must be something that is wholly clear in the modern sense of the word. But it is at the same time something that is associated with patience and inner soul-energy. And above all else there belongs to it something which no-one can give to another: that one is able to make a promise to oneself and then keep it. Once one begins to meditate, one is accomplishing the only completely free deed in this human life of ours.

Rudolf Steiner

FOREWORD

Our 'know how' has outstripped our 'know why'. On the one hand, modern technology and economic growth continue to develop apace. On the other hand, there is a rising tide of new age groups, personal growth methods and people following meditative paths. Science no longer seems to give sufficient answers to questions asked by people searching for meaning and growth.

Many young people have profound inner experiences, often without a meditative training. However, some find it difficult to understand what they are experiencing. This may be caused by a lack of preparation, the lack of maps for charting these new experiences, and because their soul forces of thinking, feeling and willing are too chaotic. This leads to the mixing up of supersensible experiences with unconscious sense perceptions. All sorts of illusions may result.

The aim of this book is to prepare the way for a clearer understanding of the fields of spiritual experiences which are opening up. The methods suggested here lead beyond the frontiers of the natural sciences in a systematic, practical way.

Jörgen Smit was born in Bergen in Norway in 1916, and taught at the Bergen Rudolf Steiner School from 1940 – 1965. He founded the Jarna Rudolf Steiner Seminar with Arne Klingborg in 1961 in Sweden – where he worked in teacher training until 1975. He then worked as the head of the Education and Youth Sections of the Anthroposophical Society at the Goetheanum in Switzerland before his death.

He ran workshops concerned with inner development

with young people in Europe, North and South America over many years. Such workshops and meetings aimed to help people find their own way, and make their own judgements since 'everyone must do it for themselves'.

Martin Large

Chapter One

Introduction: from science to the meditative path.

In the following essay the attempt will be made to illuminate through personal experiences some of the main features of the path of knowledge which Rudolf Steiner has fully and comprehensively established and developed for the present time.

The meditative path of Anthroposophy is a direct extension of the scientific method of research. For with the experimental method that is based upon sense-perceptions, as with the theories that proceed from them, one comes – with regard to the *being* of man and the world – up against inner and outer frontiers to which no satisfactory resolutions can any longer be found. The critical situation in which human beings of the present time find themselves with respect to individual and social life and to their relationship with the natural world is a clear indication of this phenomenon. This will be overcome only when, with the help of new faculties, an expansion of consciousness can arise at these frontiers of natural science. Then it will be possible for new realms of research to be opened up to human powers of cognition through the transformation of thinking, feeling and willing. Thus it is not a matter of further ingenious theories or of subjective 'mystical' feeling-experiences; what is alone decisive is whether access to the spiritually real *facts* of the world and of the human being can be found.

Every modern man is at present in a gulf, a split between his *inner experiences* and his *impressions of the outer world*. As they are in our time, neither of these is able to shed any light upon the urgent question of the being of Man. Our inner experiences, in all their individual details, represent the effects of outer experiences. If a certain element of these inner experiences is taken hold of as 'the essential reality', it dissolves with exact observation into 'illusion', or proves itself to be the sum of several outer impressions. While if, on the other hand, the contents of outer experiences are examined more closely, these are found to be coloured and influenced by various subjective elements of our inner world. On both sides there is at present a labyrinth of uncertainties, ambiguities or a total lack of clarity. Thus insofar as the question of the true being of man is concerned, one gazes – both in one's inner experiences and in the impressions one receives from the outside world – into a cognitive darkness. To be sure, there is within this double darkness a clear *feeling* of the existence of one's own being, but no adequate insight as to what this being really is – as when one knows for certain from the movements of a curtain that something is behind it, without it being possible directly to perceive and understand this something.

What, then, are the steps of a path of knowledge which leads to a union of the spiritual essence within man with the spiritual essence of the outer world, so that a gradual illumination of that darkness and an overcoming of the gulf between inner and outer may be attained? In what follows, four principal stages on this path of knowledge will be distinguished:

1. The experience of independent thinking through the illuminating and strengthening power of inner activity.
2. The development and unfolding of a living inner imagination.
3. The establishing of an 'empty' consciousness as a spiritual resonance-organ, the development of the capacity to 'hear' the spiritual.
4. The comprehending of the essence of man's inner nature and his surroundings, the gradual overcoming of the gulf between inner and outer in the realm of cognition and in social life.

Chapter Two

A concentration exercise and the control of thinking: the illuminating and strengthening of independent thinking

A first concentration-exercise assisting towards the illuminating and strengthening of the certainty of thinking can lead to important experiences.

For the purpose of this concentration-exercise one may take a quite simple object, e.g. a pocket-knife. One then concentrates for a short time, approximately five minutes, on simple thoughts that one may form in the course of observing the pocket-knife: colour, form, function, manufacture, the particular shape of the pocket-knife compared with other knives, etc. All other, irrelevant thoughts as might arise are consciously kept at a distance. It depends upon the clarity and strength of one's concentration. One takes one's thoughts only as far as one consciously determines for oneself, one thinks only of as many thoughts as one wishes to bring forth. There is neither rule nor obligation as to what and how much one is to think. It is purely a matter of one's own activity, clarity and objective certainty.

When this concentration-exercise is practised for the first time, it is perfectly possible to bring it at once to a certain degree of perfection. Everything is clear and certain, there are no disturbing thoughts interrupting the relevant train of thought. But if the same concentration-exercise is then carried out for ten days for about five minutes at a time, it is quite possible for it to be substantially worse on the tenth day than it was on the first. This is surprising at first, since one would have thought that every exercise must, with repetition, slowly become better and better. However, that is not the case. At the first attempt everything was still new and interesting, so that all one's forces were freshly harnessed and thus brought about the successful result. On the tenth occasion the sense of newness has gone and hence the enterprise is also less interesting, even a little boring. And at once there arise irrelevant, distracting thoughts which interrupt the flow of the exercise.

Thus by the tenth occasion the capacity to concentrate appears to be 'denuded', lacking the support and sustenance of what is new and interesting. The interest must now be generated anew wholly out of inner thought-forces, even though the endeavour is no longer 'new'. This leads to a heightened level of concentration, which renders one more and more independent of outer supports.

A further important experience may be described as follows. After some time one comes to regulate the course of the concentration-exercise so well that one inwardly and silently 'speaks' a long self-contained 'word-sequence'. The larynx may move, even though no sounds can be heard. At the same time, however, one is thinking of something completely different, so that one's mind becomes to a certain extent 'twin-tracked'. But this is not real concentration. The false direction will be produced through the power of one's language. If one is able to formulate something well, language very often begins to flow of its own accord, and real thought ceases as a result. Language is the best medium for the expression of thought. The essential nature of thought is, however, "language-less". A concept can also be conceived without words, and its linguistic form varies with the different languages. Thus language consolidates the original force of the thought. This 'power of language' can be overcome if one carries out the concentration-exercise anew and forbids oneself from inwardly and inaudibly 'speaking' even one single word. One can quieten one's larynx altogether and try to think wordlessly, while nevertheless grasping the thought-content of the concentration-exercise clearly and surely. This is achieved through a continuous series of inner mental images which represent all the relevant thought-content of the concentration-exercise without the use of words and which allow this to become conscious. When this has been done, one can again take up words as the means whereby thoughts are expressed – only now in full consciousness and grasped from within, so that language no longer flows along under its own momentum.

Through these concentration-exercises thinking becomes penetrated with a new strength of will. It may happen that part of this will-power shoots into the muscles, thus leading to muscular tensions in the course of concentration-exercises, for example in the throat, the neck, the scalp, the feet or the stomach – or even to manifestations of cramp. This is most certainly a sign of a wrong attitude. The will should not shoot into the muscles, for the muscles ought to be completely relaxed during concentration-exercises. The will should far rather stream into the thinking in a manner quite detached from the body.

Thinking becomes more and more independent, and arrays itself against two disturbers of the peace. On the one side the tendency towards arbitrary, will-o'-the wisp-like associations is overcome, and on the other the tendency towards compulsive thoughts is dissolved. With compulsive thoughts one is also able to hold fast to a definite thought-content, but out of compulsion. That is not thought-concentration. For this consists rather in that one dwells upon a particular thought-content only as long as this is determined by one's own inner power of thinking.

This self-sufficiency of thinking is manifested through a fine, subtle feeling of inner firmness and certainty. Rudolf Steiner recommends in his description[1] that at the conclusion of the concentration-exercise one concentrates upon this delicate feeling of inner certainty, first sensing this in the front part of the head and then, through thoughts, pouring forth this feeling into the brain and spinal cord. Clarity of thought is to be found at the surface of thinking in the 'front part' of the head. Thinking does, however, have other, deeper realms, through which clarity of thought must also gradually pass. The corresponding physical foundations for these deeper regions are the back part of the brain and the spinal cord. Through experiencing the influx of clarity of thought the will-intensity of the concentration-exercise is increased in these realms too.

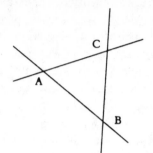

A further stage in the strengthening of independent thinking-activity may be reached through the following exercise. First, one may imagine a triangle ABC formed out of three lines of infinite length meeting in the three points A, B and C. The lines AB and AC are fixed. The line BC is then rotated around the fixed point B, so that the point C moves along the line AC. Through this means an infinite number of new triangles arise with the base AB and the angle CAB remaining constant. Then the line AC is also slowly rotated around the fixed point A – in such a way that with each of such smaller movements the line BC makes one complete rotation around point B. From this we get an endless number of infinitely many triangles. Finally the point B is allowed to move to infinity along the line AB. With each slight movement of this point the line AC is allowed to make one complete rotation around point A and with each movement of the line AC the line BC revolves once around point B – which is itself moving along the line AB. This yields an infinity of an endless number of infinitely many triangles. If this – or another similar geometrical line-movement of one's own invention – is calmly and consistently carried out, with one's eyes shut, one will be able inwardly to perceive a strong thinking activity. The more clearly and the more intensively the details of the line-movements are perceived in thought, so much the more clearly can one's own thinking-activity be grasped as *supersensible, spiritual perception*. A prerequisite for this first supersensible perception is that the line-movements do not remain in nebulous general thoughts but are imagined, through inner strength, in an altogether concrete manner (not only as a 'formal' mathematical definition) and that inner attention is then directed with strength and determination upon this activity.

Generating colour images

The following exercise forms a further stage of this growth towards a supersensible perception. One paints a red circle of colour and then a circular area of green around the red circle, and beside it, in contrast, a green circle of colour surrounded by a circular area of red. As one contemplates these two areas of colour, one generates a continuous inner flow from one coloured image to the other and back again. One can perceive this inner picturing activity clearly within. When this exercise has first been done with one's eyes open, it can be repeated with one's eyes closed. The point of this is inwardly to generate radiantly strong colour-images in the course of this regular movement. Thereby one's own picturing activity will be still more clearly perceived.[2]

Capacities for this inner beholding of colour-images vary considerably with each individual. Some people maintain that they would be quite unable to see any colour-images in this way, even with the greatest effort. In this exercise they would merely think that the colour was red (or green), but they would only see the letters forming the word *red* and not the colour. While others have radiant colour-experiences without the slightest effort. There are people who see manifestations of colour in total darkness without any pressure on the eye – and this even from childhood. With this exercise, however, it is not a matter of what inner capacities one has already but, rather, of the strength of the effort that one needs consciously to add something to what one has.

If even with great exertion one sees mere letters rather than inner colours, there are some preliminary exercises that can be done which eventually give rise to inner colour-images. One very simple such exercise is to gaze at a red or green coloured surface and in thus gazing to try to feel the quality of the colour so strongly that one inwardly becomes quite 'red' or 'green'. Then one shuts one's eyes, while inwardly retaining this pure qualitative feeling. And from this feeling one can, with eyes closed, generate the inner, radiant colour-image. If this does not work, the same exercise is repeated and supplemented by other appropriate colour-exercises. In order that one comes to feel the pure quality of colour, one to some extent *absorbs* it into oneself. If nothing is felt in this way, then neither can the colour-quality be absorbed. The inner colour-image is then generated from the strength of the feeling for the colour-quality. This preliminary exercise may also be broadened: one gazes into the blue sky until one clearly experiences the inner feeling-quality of the blue. Then one shuts one's eyes and allows the inner image of the blue sky to rise up out of this strong feeling. Similarly with a green meadow, a pine- or birch-forest, a roaring, surging sea, or a mountain-summit. With every outward sense-impression there is a corresponding echo in one's feelings. The inner, colour-filled image is generated from out of this definite quality-laden feeling. In our time we all too easily slip from one impression to the next and thus always remain on the surface – or we confuse the impressions that come from without with our personally determined feelings, and a clear, distinct feeling does not arise.

Such preliminary exercises are suitable not only for those who are wholly unable to bring forth inner colour-images. They are at the present time of pressing importance for almost every person, since through our busy lifestyle there develops the ever more common tendency to experience the world in a grey, superficial manner – with the result that the world of one's inner experience becomes equally grey. One may see this for oneself if one first looks at a red rose with one's eyes open and then, shutting one's eyes, brings forth an inner image of the red rose. Now the two roses are compared with one another: which of the two has the stronger colours? With most people the rose that one beholds with open eyes will have stronger colours than the image that has been conceived inwardly. However, this does not need to remain so. The colour-intensity of the inner image can even be strengthened to the extent that it becomes stronger than that of the rose which is seen with one's eyes open. This greater intensity does not, however, arise solely through exertions of the will. First, there must be a deepened, calm *feeling* for the quality of the senses. Both the attentiveness that is concentrated outwards and the devotion focussed upon the deepened feeling are then generated by the will. The result is that the strong inner colour-image appears.

If, in this way, one has done some preliminary exercises, the exercise with the alternating colour-images will become ever clearer. Now the possibility arises for a direct perception of this inner activity. This requires a strong, purposefully directed attentiveness. One then experiences the active reality of thinking, which in every conceptual act is unconscious and remains in the background. In ordinary thinking only the shadowy, abstract end-results become conscious. The perception of a deeper level in the reality of thinking is a supersensible experience.

Through this step the normal consciousness of every day is, in two respects, broadened, supplemented and fructified. Initially we have to do with an instinctively forged conception that is compounded from abstract and shadowy thought-content and from *dried up*, phantom-like sense experiences. Through the inwardly active strengthening of pure thinking-activity this can consciously be held back. Sense-experiences are thereby freed from the mental pictures with which they are otherwise enshrouded and appear in their original, pure strength and fullness. The more strongly and the more purely that sense-perceptions can be experienced, so much the more clearly can a thinking evolve that is not bound to sense-experiences. The strength of pure thinking, in its turn, makes possible a pure drinking in of unclouded sense-qualities. It is like a pendulum, which can slowly increase its swing on either side. It is like out-breathing and in-breathing. The more strongly and fully one breathes out, the better one is able to breathe in.

Wonder

Herewith, an essential faculty for advancing in knowledge is partly rediscovered and partly generated anew: this is the faculty of wonder. All children, to a greater or lesser extent, possess this faculty. In the course of adult life this faculty is, however, all too often dulled and weakened through habit, routine and conventional ideas. People believe they know how things are. The original sense of wonder has been lost. Only in exceptional cases does it re-appear. In reality, wonder is the prerequisite of every new sense-impression, every new thought-stimulus and, consequently, every new perception. As soon as fixed mental images come in place of wonder, the living activity of cognition dies. For this reason, a re-enlivening and re-discovering of childhood wonder on a higher level is a necessity, while a deepening and strengthening of this faculty – such as is not yet possible with children – is also now required. On this path a new quality of inner imagination will gradually be attained, and this leads to a next step along the path of knowledge. As a means of clarifying this process, the following exercise is particularly suitable.

The observation of growing and withering plants.

One is enjoined to observe, in the plant kingdom, on the one hand the budding, sprouting life and the thriving, blossoming exuberance of plants, and, alternating with this, their fading, withering decay. This depends on a direct observation and unconditioned devotion to what is going on within nature. One should not feel or think anything beforehand but, rather, observe through one's open senses all that is coming towards one. Only after such observation do feelings and thoughts appear which correspond in a wholly appropriate way with what is going on in Nature. One sees, for example, how the little light-green birch-leaf grows in complete oneness with the warmth of the sun, with the light and with the dampness in the air, so that every smallest part of the birch-leaf is in harmony with the whole leaf and with the whole tree and with the whole environment. Then one sees how the fading leaves disintegrate on the ground, so that every smallest part of the fading leaf loses its connection with the other parts, and how the same environment of warmth, light and air which furthers the growth of the sprouting leaf accelerates the dying of the fading leaf. In the delicate forms of the fading leaf one may still observe the vestiges of the life that has been. These two processes of sprouting and fading now themselves begin slowly to speak in the inner regions of the soul. Definite and quite diverse feelings spring up within the soul.

This is a decisive point in this exercise. In his description Rudolf Steiner refers to it thus:

'New kinds of feelings and thoughts, *which one has not known before,* will be seen to arise within one's soul.'[3]

What can these words mean? One has had definite feelings and thoughts regarding sprouting and fading within nature ever since childhood. Hence, these are not the feelings referred to here. It is a question of considering feelings and thoughts of a kind such as one has not previously known. Everyone initially mixes his personal feelings, which proceed from his bodily state and life-situation, with his feelings regarding his natural environment. Personal grief or joy mingle unobserved with one's relationship to nature. These are the *old* kind of feelings, which are already familiar. In this exercise it is a matter of withholding and stilling these personal feelings and of allowing only those feelings which arise directly out of contemplation of both natural processes to hold sway. These pure feelings, as they are unclouded by personal associations, are at first still weak but they gradually become *clearer* and *more definite.* Every

feeling of this kind has an unequivocal gesture; the feeling of
sprouting is different from the feeling of fading. Can these
various feelings be described more precisely? Rudolf Steiner
here offers a hint from which a great deal can be learnt:

> 'It is possible to describe with a certain degree of accuracy
> what these feelings are like. Anyone who has these inner
> experiences can form for himself an integral picture of
> them. Whoever has directed his attention towards the
> process of becoming, thriving and blossoming will feel
> something that is *distantly similar* to the experience of a
> sunrise; while the process of fading and dying will give rise
> in him to an experience which, in the same way, may be
> compared in one's mental horizon with the slow rising of
> the moon.' [4]

Two experiences of two entirely different natural phenomena
are here brought together with the living feelings of sprouting
and growing and of fading and dying that have already been
observed. These four experiences or feelings now begin mutually
to clarify and deepen themselves, and to shed light upon each
other – as in an inner language formed out of the images of
experience.

It is not being suggested that sprouting is the sun or the
sunrise, or that fading is the moon or the rising of the moon.
These are two experiences which are compared with the two
feelings. Thinking's mobile attentiveness can, however, bring
these together only if the four feeling-experiences are sufficiently
strong. Then the spiritual facts which work through the
gestures underlying these feelings speak through the picture-
language. Every living picture is born out of feeling.

In what form does this picture-language of experience first
appear? It first emerges just as one's childhood-memories do,
that is, when one is oneself directly inside the picture. At each
moment it is generated anew.

There is a further, inner experience which can be described
as follows. With these two feeling-experiences in the back-

ground, one may contemplate one's own thinking. This now appears in such a way that growing and thriving and withering and fading are also present in our own thinking. Thinking is only possible if every thought flows out of the totality of thought-possibilities and if it maintains a living connection with these endlessly many thought-possibilities. A thought which is completely separated from all other thoughts would immediately lose its own thought-content. Every thought whose content is real lives through the grace of the totality of thinking. But all thinking must – if the necessary clarity is to be attained – also acquire outlines, emphasize differences and aspire to clear definition; it needs the supportive sheath of a contoured form. If, however, this outweighs the livingness of the thought, something in thinking begins to fade until only dead formulations and definitions remain – which, as they become more fixed and separate, actually come to lose both clarity and content.

Thus in thinking both these fundamental gestures are present, the ascending and the descending, blossoming and fading. Natural processes may be discovered anew within man. The gulf between inner and outer that was referred to at the outset has begun, in one first step, to be overcome.

Chapter Three

The inner faculty of imagination as a part of the quest for knowledge: exercises on the path towards Imagination

The inner faculty of imagining originates in direct association with sense-perceptions. The inner movements of colour-surfaces has as its content the same as what was perceived with one's own eyes. However, it needs to be raised to a higher level if it is to be freed from this direct connection to the sense-perception: the symbolic image. The following exercise can elucidate the manifoldness of the possibilities that exist here. The exercise has three phases: preparation, in which some kind of coherence is built up through thought-content, the meditation proper, wherein the symbolic image that has been constructed through the preparation lives with inner strength in the soul, and an after-effect whereby what has been yielded through the meditation works on in feeling.

Looking backwards and forwards

First one looks back over the events of the past few days, as a whole as well as in detail. Then one directs one's attention to the events and deeds which will probably come in the course of the next few days. Then one conceives of this picture as being extended in both directions. In this way a complete biography would gradually result. If this exercise has been carried through to a certain point one may say to oneself: This is only one part of the real course of my life. For I have omitted to take into account all that occurs in the deep sleep of night. Only through the processes that occur in the depths of sleep are the experiences and deeds of the day possible. Not only the nightly refreshment that follows the weariness of evening but also the deepening, clarifying and digesting of the experiences of the previous day, the new impulses for the next day, spring from the deep sleep of night. Now one may try to concentrate upon the nightly periods of deep sleep and to call these to consciousness in one stream that flows through the whole of life. These two streams, the day-stream and the stream of deep sleep, are both equally important for life. Now the course of life can only rightly be grasped if attention is directed towards the purely *individual* power of human development. Thus there will be an awareness of *how* man develops further through the combined working of the day-stream and the stream of deep sleep. When these three fundamental aspects, these three streams, have been grasped in the course of life through thoughts, one may present them in the form of a symbolic line-drawing:

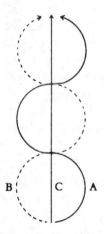

The day-stream of the course of life is represented by the curved line A; the stream of deep sleep by the dotted line B and the individual stream of development by the middle line C.[5] After the introductory phase of building up the thought-picture, the meditation proper now follows. One lives inwardly in the simple, symbolic image of the three lines. This symbolic image can be seen inwardly before one. The meditation acquires greater power if one feels oneself fully into the picture, into the forces streaming through the three lines, so that one creates the three lines for oneself in every moment. This is comparable with the way in which our memories rise spontaneously to the surface – except that here is no memory-picture but rather an image generated in freedom.

If the meditation is carried out to the end, one can let the sense of reality that has been generated resound in one's feelings. One then contemplates the familiar daily course in an altogether new way. This familiar daily course loses none of its significance thereby; but it comes to be experienced in a much more coherent way. While the outer course of the day tends otherwise to be regarded all too easily as the *whole* of life, our perception of this phenomenon is now widened through every feeling. This forms a step on the path from everyday consciousness to the new heights and depths of our own essential reality.

The symbol that has been built up here is the well-known, ancient symbol of the Mercury staff, which has been used over several centuries in various connections and with a diversity of meanings. With the present meditation it is of no consequence whether one knows anything about these old, historical connections or not. All that matters is one's own spiritual strength, which is summoned forth through the preparatory, synthesizing weaving of thoughts and then through the concentrated power of the meditation generated by dwelling upon the symbolic image of the lines. Through the symbolic structure of this meditation a still deeper power is awakened than in the exercise with the moving coloured images referred to above. There is a sense-free element in that exercise too, through the strength of movement of the coloured images. In the meditation of the symbolic image with the three lines this sense-free element comes more and more strongly to the fore.

Wisdom lives in the light

The content of the meditation can be a symbolic image such as is first built up through the weaving of thoughts and then evolves as an inner picturing activity. The meditation can, however, also be stimulated through words. An example of such a word-meditation is:

Wisdom lives in the light.[6]

The preconditions for this meditation vary considerably from person to person. With some it can lead after only a short time to decisive spiritual experiences. With others nothing at all happens at first. What matters with this meditation is the spiritual power which the individual generates in the meditation, the power with which she develops her thoughts. For this very reason there is no definite content which could be brought to the meditator's attention so as to tell her what she should be thinking. The point is that she must generate these for herself. However, it is possible to indicate a *preliminary step* which, though not the meditation itself, can nevertheless lead to the point at which the meditation *begins*.

This could be described as follows. One is in a forest at night. The sky is covered with clouds, and total darkness reigns. It is impossible to see anything of one's surroundings. Slowly, however, comes the dawn, until the radiant daylight brings the whole surroundings into view in all their forms and colours. How would it be now if light did not exist and eternal night would reign? One concentrates upon these thoughts. Then one allows the thoughts of the dawn to arise once more. The essential significance of light, through which everything is able to come into view, becomes clear. Then one imagines an utterly confused, absurd social- or rather antisocial- situation: misunderstandings between old friends, completely incomprehensible deeds on the part of others and completely incomprehensible misinterpretations of one's own intentions: social darkness. One then lets the dawn of knowledge enter the situation. Everything is gradually clarified and appears in its true form. Then one allows social darkness to enter in again in one's thoughts and one imagines that this will last for ever because the light of knowledge does not exist. Then the enlightening power of knowledge is again allowed to appear. The essential significance of the light of knowledge thereby becomes clear.

When one has called these two situations to mind, one joins them together and compares the outer light of the Sun with the inner light of knowledge. This is the same fact approached from two sides. The oneness of the quality of light forms a bridge between inner and outer and, hence, a basis for our meditation.

The content of this preparatory step is *not* identical with the meditation. However, through this preparatory step it is possible to arrive at the point where the meditation 'Wisdom lives in the light', *begins*.

If one succeeds in leaving sense-experience aside, these words may form a door through which one may enter into spiritual *activity*. This activity is completely individual and its content cannot be prescribed. Moreover, a certain unconditional inner effort of will is required and through this one's whole individual existence is set into action. When rightly carried out, there appears with this meditation the feeling of a certain independence from one's outward bodily foundation, one begins to have an intimation of one's own self in its true form. This gives rise to a clear feeling – which is itself, to be sure, quite secondary to the meditation – of *hovering*. Whence comes this feeling?

In the familiar consciousness of every-day one has a natural, and quite convincing, feeling that one is not hovering. One stands on the ground and feels the force of gravity as pressure under the feet or – in sitting – pressure under the thighs. In all these perceptions in the realm of touch our will-power works in harness with gravity. During the meditation this will-power is drawn away from the sense-organs and is led over into the spiritual activity of the meditation. So long as this condition lasts, the corresponding sense-perceptions actually cease. Thus in this situation one has no perceptions in the realm of touch and hence no sense of gravity, that is, one experiences oneself to be hovering. It is the same with other physical sense-perceptions. For example, one also *hears* nothing. This can be observed especially clearly at the transition from meditation to ordinary consciousness. Then for a few seconds the gentlest rustling of leaves in the forest – if, that is, the meditation has been carried out (on a bench) in a wood – is like the raging of a storm. It lasts only seconds, because the power of understanding then immediately takes its place again in the brain and imbues all sense-perceptions with ideas which order and dampen them down. Children sometimes have the same experience directly before they go to sleep. The ordering power of understanding has drawn itself out a little, and the child still has aural perceptions which then appear, undimmed and uncontrolled, as loud roaring when the bedcover is gently moved.

An ordered transition from the meditation to ordinary every-day consciousness is in many respects especially important. First of all there emerges a strange feeling: ordinary consciousness appears confined and hence is set in the context of something greater – for it is no longer the only thing that exists. It does, however, lose nothing of its existential significance thereby. For only through this initial circumstance of ordinary consciousness is an independent, free power of judgement possible. For that reason it should never be obliterated. It is comparable to the sure place of anchorage of a ship in harbour, which can always be left again for passages across the sea. Many people of today – especially young people – have so great a spiritual endowment and inclination that they come very quickly to the experience of 'hovering'. It can be so strong that a fear then arises of thereby losing oneself and of not being able to 'come back'. A slow and patient strengthening of the soul-forces, of the ordering, concentrating power of the ego, is then imperative in order that this fear – which is at first perfectly well-founded and justified – may be overcome. Only in such a way can the expansion of consciousness be carried through without any danger.

In ordinary every-day consciousness, thinking, feeling and

willing are constantly corrected through the laws of the outer physical world. Every false step is for the most part noticed at once. Hence in the course of life it follows that there is an outwardly supported certainty in one's consciousness. Now with the expansion of consciousness on the meditative path of knowledge a similar certainty and solidity has to be developed without this outer support. Inner spiritual activity must therefore be strengthened to such an extent that the pendulum-swing, the 'breathing' between pure thinking and pure perception (which was described above) becomes possible. For this reason it represents a higher stage in the ordinary independence and certainty of human consciousness. It is at the same time a higher stage in the ordinary breathing-process, the in-breathing and out-breathing of air. This higher stage consists of an out-breathing and in-breathing in pure thinking and pure perception; it is a 'light-soul-process'![7]

Ordinary consciousness is protected and supported from without in the three-dimensional realm. The higher stage of the light-soul-process unfolds in a *time-organism*. Here, time becomes 'space'. Whatever proceeds in small and greater rhythms of time is grasped as a wholeness. The whole is present in every small part, and the smallest part is in harmony with the whole. This time-organism is the field of life. Through the expansion of consciousness and the faculty of knowledge such as has been described, a new faculty – which may be termed *formative thinking* – develops in one's thinking in addition to the analytical, critical faculty which in ordinary consciousness must first be extensively practised and developed and which endows it with certainty. This faculty has the task of generating from within the forms arising in life's process of becoming and in the time-organism with the same certainty with which analytical thinking grasps points in space or any particular fragment of time.

CHAPTER FOUR

Empty Consciousness – the awakening of the spiritual organs of perception: exercises on the path towards Inspiration

With the development of an imaginative, formative thinking in which strengthened thinking works together with a pure perceptive faculty, a significant step has been made towards the overcoming of the gulf between subject and object, between inner and outer. This means initially a significant strengthening and expanding of the active forces of one's own being, and leads to a certain onesidedness and limitation which can be overcome only through a further stage.

Of what does this limitation consist? Every person brings to their development certain colourings, peculiarities and one-sidednesses, while they lack certain qualities altogether – a fact that they often do not themselves notice. Far from being counteracted by the strengthening and expanding of consciousness, this one-sidedness is at first increased still further.

The next stage consists of 'withdrawing' this whole strengthening of forces. The spiritual world that lies beyond subject and object should speak within one's being, it should become heard and received. At the same time the soul, the ego, must learn to be silent. It is a path towards the overcoming of egoism. This path must begin in everyday life. Every deed of true love goes a small way towards overcoming egoism. Every selfless, beneficent and self-sacrificing deed represents a short distance towards this goal. But any person with a bit of self-knowledge knows that a large part of egoism nevertheless remains unconsciously present. If this is to be overcome, a heightening of the capacity to love is necessary, and to begin with this can be attained through cognitive activity. There are in this respect an especially large number of misunderstandings at the present time. It will be said, for example: Whoever wishes to attain insights into the supersensible, spiritual or divine must obliterate his own ego. This argument is convincing, but it contains only half the truth. Frequently, however, a half-truth is more misleading than a complete untruth, because it cannot be seen through so easily. If the ego – as it begins to participate – is suppressed or even obliterated, the individual thereby loses his independence. He becomes dependent upon an outside power, a 'guru' or another person, he becomes the plaything of uncontrolled forces which more or less determine what he does. The resultant position of natural egoism is then made even worse. The independence of the individual should at the present time never be surrendered – and least of all where truth and knowledge are involved. Thus the problem is much more weighty, for one's active soul-forces and the ordering powers of the ego must first be strengthened. But then the ego must, through 'withdrawing', consciously create a hollow space, become inwardly completely silent and form a receptive 'shell' which can become a resonance-organ for the spiritual world. The ego is silent, but the 'shell' that is formed in this way is inwardly strong. If a person who has only feebly cultivated his thinking and has not expanded his knowledge is silent, this silence is empty. If, on the other hand, another person, who has gained a lot of knowledge through strength of thinking, holds himself back, is silent and listens, he can likewise perceive much and hear with penetration. The shell that is formed from such hearing is a resonance-organ which leads to a spiritual 'hearing'; and this is referred to as 'empty' consciousness.

Rediscovering sound and hearing

There are many preparatory exercises which lead to this decisive step of spiritual *inspiration*. An attentive rediscovering of ordinary, physical hearing is indispensable here. The sound-colours of the various things and substances have within them endless depths, which would not be noticed by a superficial hearing. How do the different kinds of wood, the various metals and stones, sound? How does water rush, how differently does the wind whisper in the leaves of an oak than in an elm, how does the wind murmur in the depths of a pine-forest? All these sound-colours are, again, essentially different from the sound-colours which are imbued with soul-forces – as, for instance, the well contented grunting of a pig eating or the cry of anguish when the same pig is slaughtered. Where a soul-gesture is perceived through the sound-colour, a large field of hearing is opened up: for in such a case hearing extends far beyond the physical-acoustic realm. If one returns again from this field of hearing to the sound-colours of the woods and metals etc., where there is no resounding from the conscious realms of soul, these sound-colours also begin to reveal new depths.

These perception-exercises in the realm of hearing form an indispensable preliminary stage for spiritual hearing, where the strengthened ego can hold itself back to such an extent that spiritual, inner 'tones', and subsequently also the spiritual 'word', can be perceived.

Nevertheless, the *self-assertive*, spiritual egoism which really only wants to listen to itself is much stronger than one supposes at first. The entire strength of this egoism manifests itself in stages. Hence there is a need for a disciplined, thorough study of one's own life-history.

Reviewing one's life history

In this review, or *Rückschau*, one may choose any situation which has placed before one a particular test and where it was necessary to develop courage and endurance. Difficulties, impediments, defeats, illness, social disappointments or attacks may have piled up from outside. Now one tries to consider all that has happened from a higher vantage-point, as though one were a different person. This is, in fact, not particularly difficult, for every person bears within him a kind of inner observer who is able to contemplate everything that occurs with a certain aloofness and objectivity. The whole is examined from above as one would a play in which one is taking part at the same time.

Taking the next step is, however, much more difficult: *to distinguish the essential from the inessential*. This can at first seem unattainable, even meaningless – for I surely cannot single out parts of the process as inessential, as everything would otherwise have taken a different course. A key which offers a way forward from here is the following question: Which forces for development have been formed as a result of the process? If courage or endurance have increased, this is decisive for the whole of the life that follows and obviously of greater significance than the incidental content of the episodes. The strides of development that one takes as a result of such events are always more significant than the substance of the events themselves.

In the course of this search for the very essence of one's own destiny, when one can become conscious of a new depth in one's existence, one necessarily discovers a series of other people whose presence in the immediate vicinity was absolutely necessary for a certain incident. This becomes especially clear if one gradually expands one's life-study from the situation selected initially to a complete review of one's life. The people who participated in one's destiny seem to one's conscious mind as it is engaged in the *Rückschau* as at first of less significance than one's own person. One does, so to speak, *oneself* play the principal part in the theatre of life, the others being mere *supernumeraries*. In this image one's hidden egoism expresses itself clearly. When one becomes conscious of this, one is at first thoroughly frightened. Through this means the relative importance of the existence of other people and oneself is reversed. For the contemplative consciousness the significance of one's own personality is now immaterial, one lives in one's consciousness only in the being of the others. They appear as the true reality, while this feeling for the reality of one's own personality disappears. What would one have become without the decisive advice of a teacher, how would one's life have proceeded if a certain misfortune had not sharply awakened one out of a phase of lethargy, what would one have been without parents and friends, without brothers and sisters and relatives? Would one's existence not have become completely nullified without these decisive influences from one's fellow-men? If one deducts these from one's capacity for development, one will see how little of what one had formerly regarded as one's own qualities still remains. The supposed self proves to be a total illusion. This is a crucial step, for only when one's transient personality has altogether receded into the background can the ego that is the source of freedom, of independent judgement and love, be found. This is found simultaneously as higher self, within one's own being and in the other person. The higher self lives simultaneously in the centre and in the periphery.

This intensive study of one's biography can, by way of practice, begin with a concrete, short episode and then gradually expand to one's whole life. The expansion must, however, always be accomplished in a concrete and content-orientated way. The more precisely this is carried out for every year of one's life, so much the more strongly will egoism recede. It will not, however, be dismissed in a moment. If one says to oneself: 'From now on I shall not be egoistic any more', that is, of course, mere self-deception. Only through the concrete discovery of the essential significance of other people – for one's whole life, year by year – will egoism be overcome.

Through the rediscovering and contemplation of the surrounding circle of one's fellow men one's relationship to one's natural environment is also widened. Thus insofar as one's higher self lives in others, so is it also active in one's natural surroundings – especially in those of childhood. However, this will become conscious only if the aforementioned exercises for the deepening of sense-perceptions, colours and tones and of the whole fullness of nature have progressed sufficiently far. Otherwise one's natural environment will be experienced more or less as a pale outward show. Nonetheless, it is in all its forces really no less a factor in one's destiny than the forces of the human beings with whom we are connected. Did I spend my childhood amongst high mountains, in a pine-forest, by a stormy sea or in a city? The higher self can be found in one's innermost depths, but always at the same time also in meetings with other people and at deeper levels of one's perceptions of nature.

The path towards the overcoming of egoism is steep and stony. Many specific little exercises can serve as support here. One example is the following.

Observing habits and gestures

One sets out to observe oneself with regard to little, essentially insignificant habits, gestures which one often makes unconsciously, or favourite words which one frequently uses in a striking way. One chooses one of these habits and resolves not to employ this gesture or favourite word during the coming months and in its stead to use another gesture or another word. One may then have two interesting experiences. The resistance to altering in-grained habits, even if they seem to be devoid of meaning, is much greater than anticipated. It is as though a strong force asserted itself in these habits which would say: 'Under no circumstances will I change'. The second experience is, however, still more important: It is possible to change, to transform oneself, it is possible to act out of resolve and insight. The sense of freedom that is acquired through a transformation which one brings about and fashions consciously for oneself is most beneficial for one's further development.

Controlling the will

The next step is an exercise for controlling the will. One invents for oneself a little action that one carries out the next day at a definite time. The action should not form part of one's normal activities or social duties, nor should it have any direct practical use.

When thus completely detached from these necessities there

is nothing that could give rise to such an act other than one's free initiative. In carrying it out one dwells upon the power of resolution which gives rise to the deed. Both with this exercise, as with the changing of habits, one subconsciously experiences a delicate sense of sorrow, which can then also become conscious. This forms part of every self-conquest. As self-mastery grows in strength, so too does this sense of sorrow. Just at the stage of knowledge where the strengthened ego withdraws, thus establishing the hollow space, or 'empty' consciousness, this sorrow plays a large part. It is for this reason that this stage of knowledge is not at first generally reached, for one subconsciously wishes to avoid sorrow. The nearer one gets to this stage, the more does the sorrow grow. But courage and the desire for truth and knowledge can also, correspondingly, grow as the means of mastering cowardice and helping to bear these sorrows. Every real advance in the life of knowledge is born of sorrow.

The civilisation of the present has a fundamentally dismissive attitude towards sorrow, even though it does itself bring about immense sorrow. To avoid sorrow, men use narcotics and seek out ways of diverting it. Our civilisation strives after pleasure and comfort, while there has on the other hand never been a civilisation which has tortured and killed so many people. Superficiality and pleasure seeking are but two symptoms of this situation.

It is not a question of sorrow for its own sake or of some kind of self-torment and asceticism. That would not be appropriate. The function of sorrow on the path of knowledge must be rightly understood. Man needs the feeling of genuine pleasure and true joy, for it works like wind in the sails of the ship of life. But sorrow belongs unquestioningly to every higher stage of *consciousness*. It is an essential accompanying phenomenon – though the courage that leads to knowledge and further development must be stronger. If this is not the case, sorrow can work only crushingly and destructively. The error of the ascetic lies in believing that sorrow can of itself have an elevating effect. The sorrow referred to here is like birth-pangs. What really matters is always the 'child' that is in the process of becoming.

Looking back over the day

A further exercise that strengthens the power of self-conquest is the daily evening-review (*Rückschau*) of the day that is coming to an end. For this purpose the course of events and experiences is followed in reverse order, so that one begins with the last event before going to sleep and finishes with getting up in the morning. In addition, every event can itself also be contemplated in reverse. It is at first hardly possible to achieve a complete review of the whole day. The complete review will initially be carried out only with respect to a small period, while the remaining time will be lumped together in one great panorama. Gradually the small period may become greater. The reversed direction in the *Rückschau* is important for the reason that one thereby tears oneself away from the customary forward rush from event to event and thus sees one's actions on a deeper level. One can view oneself more from the outward aspect or rather from the vantage-point of one's inner experiences.

All these exercises lead to the opening up of a new field of cognitive activity in one's thinking. This is the capacity of passing from one viewpoint to a completely opposite viewpoint, without obliterating the experiences and perceptions which one has arrived at initially. Tensions thereby arise between the different positions. There begins a 'conversation' through which something higher can play in. One's thinking becomes sufficiently mobile to adjust to the changing positions. However, there only too easily arises at this stage the misconception that thinking must here be excluded so that a higher spiritual power may speak, that all thinking is of no consequence here because each individual viewpoint must always remain one-sided. The blotting out of thinking rests for the most part upon indolence or upon a perceptual nihilism and has nothing to do with what is being presented here. Thinking remains far rather the indispensable support on the path from the simplest sense-perceptions in the physical realm to the highest spiritual realities. Without thinking, any quest for truth is in vain. Thinking must, however, develop new possibilities at each stage of knowledge; perception undergoes a transformation from one stage to another.

In the course of this development harsh discords frequently arise in a man's soul-life, for there are great possibilities and capacities which may to some extent proclaim themselves long before the individual is able to bring them into effect in his life. If, however, this is penetrated with sufficient clarity, there is no need for a loss of either peace or composure.

Cultivating calmness & composure

From the first step of the path of knowledge onwards, this 'inner peace' must be regularly cultivated. Herein lies a continuing, and fundamental, exercise on the meditative path.

Inner peace is at first difficult to grasp, for its opposite, unrest shows itself just when it is least wanted. There are the most diverse varieties of unrest: it arises through anger, becoming offended, fear, ambition, envy, vanity, overzealousness, a sense of shame, despair, an inferiority complex, megalomania, stress, a longing for sensation, stage-fright, inordinate desires; etc. Each variety of unrest has its particular colouring. The counterweight to this is, however, not phlegmatic calm, for this is further from real peace than all these varieties of unrest and consists simply in being oblivious to what is going on around one. It is of course necessary first to notice something and to awaken from one's sleepy calm. But in order then to overcome unrest, one must first examine to which type of unrest one has a tendency. Then one may imagine an extreme, though fictitious, situation, where one falls into such a state of unrest. Because one can recognise the reason for the unrest, the active kind of peace is enabled to re-establish itself in one's consciousness. The stormy waves which one has generated inwardly are made smooth again. Peace is an active force which proceeds out of man's innermost core. It must permeate our whole existence with its warmth. Passive, purely phlegmatic, peace may be cold-blooded. True peace always proceeds from the heart.

Every stage of knowledge brings one in contact with ever new stormy forces of the world-drama. Unrest must every time again be overcome. Nevertheless, the power of peace grows with each step in knowledge. If this is not the case, it is necessary to take a step backwards until the strengthened power of peace begins to work.

In stepping forward on the path of knowledge we can perceive a law, which is valid even with the first steps and then manifests itself ever more clearly. For such progress runs its course in three phases, wherein two different tendencies or types may be distinguished.

There are people who are full of strength and make themselves felt in their surroundings. In doing so they hardly change at all and remain essentially as they are. Impressions from without seem to have no particular effect on them. They could be compared to a huge rubber-ball. If such a person receives an impression from without, he will have regained his own form after a short while. We may – in the present context – term such a tendency 'positive'.[8] The opposite tendency is just as common. Outer impressions leave enduring traces, even though the individual himself has not really shaped these forms. He seems to be a copy of outer influences. Such a person could be compared to soft wax. In this context we could term such a tendency 'negative'. Only in rare exceptional cases do these one-sided types manifest themselves in so extreme a form, but the inclination towards one of these two directions may be perceived in everyone.

It is, however, altogether different when these two tendencies are not in sole authority but alternate in one and the same person, for new possibilities open up here through the power of spiritual development. In every learning-process there is something of this alternation between the two tendencies. At first there is a certain 'positive' power and capacity. But then the individual holds back everything that he knew and could do at the start and opens himself up to entirely new experiences. These can make a deep impression. But the individual does not allow himself to be determined and fixed by this one impression only. It is *assimilated* through his own forces and is finally wholly united with his essential being. Three phases, therefore, manifest themselves here: first the 'positive' forces, then the 'negative' attitude, then again a 'positive force (though on a higher level). What takes place in this way in every learning-process and in every step in man's development may be perceived on a larger and wider scale in the development towards higher stages of knowledge. It does not simply go forward in a linear fashion. First an inner strengthening must take place: the individual becomes 'positive'. Now follows the reverse tendency – the selfless receiving of something completely new through a 'negative' attitude. Only then is the third stage possible: the independent uniting of one's being with what has been newly recognised – a higher stage of the 'positive' attitude.

At the first stage the power of will – which is otherwise sleeping – is, in thinking, awakened to life, to a vibrant forming activity. At the second stage the light of consciousness is, through change and transformation in the course of life, imparted to the otherwise sleeping, unconscious will-life. At the third stage both tendencies unite in a conscious swing of the pendulum. The first phase is the stage of Imagination. The second phase is the stage of Inspiration. In the third phase the stage of Intuition becomes a reality.

Chapter 5

The integration of the higher being: exercises on the path to Intuition

Even the simplest thought – insofar as one understands the thought and does not merely repeat empty words – contains intuition, the revelation of a spiritual reality which cannot be comprehended through physical sense-organs. This spiritual reality which presents itself to conceptual thinking as intuition may be represented pictorially as the seed of a plant. The seed has within itself the germ of the whole plant, though the whole plant is not materially developed in the actual form of the seed. As the seed relates to the fully developed plant, so does the intuition that is present in the simplest of conceptual thinking relate to the fully evolved stage of Intuition, which is attainable only when the stages of Imagination and Inspiration have been sufficiently developed.

Even though the stage of true Intuition is very far from every-day consciousness, there are nonetheless exercises which are possible at a very early point in the meditative path of knowledge and which lead to Intuition – as, for example, the one which follows.

Picturing a person as complete, in the process of becoming, and as an empty canvas.

One attempts inwardly to form for oneself three pictures of another person. These three pictures should, however, be fundamentally different from one another. In the first picture one tries to draw together everything that one knows about the other person, his whole manner of being, abilities, habits, behaviour, etc., all this as a complete picture of his individuality painted as a harmonious whole. Whereas this first picture is a finished, complete picture, the second picture must of necessity be an unfinished picture, which is still in the process of arising – the painter is, so to speak, just about to take the picture further. In a meeting with another person it happens all too often that one exclusively considers the first picture, which does not necessarily correspond with the reality. One is then speaking not with the person who is present but with the picture – which is maybe even false – of his past. However well one may have comprehended the other person through the first picture, this can never give an impression of what is going on in any particular moment. This second picture to emerge is therefore different not merely with respect to its content but in that it has a fundamentally different character. For the forming of the first picture all one's inner forces must be awakened, in order that the image of the other individuality can, as it arises, be completed through the formative force of living thinking. It is not defined through outer causes but is viewed as the formed expression of spiritual wisdom. It is an experience towards the stage of Imagination.

This will not suffice for the second picture. The inner, picture-forming forces must here be withdrawn so as to create an opening for that which at every moment newly resounds and speaks forth from out of the being of the other person. It is, therefore, an exercise leading towards the stage of Inspiration.

The third picture is the most difficult, but also the most important. It is not finished or formed complete out of the past. Nor is it even in process of becoming. In this case, the painter has, so to speak, not yet begun to paint the picture. All that one has before one is the painter, the empty canvas and the paint-pots – there is nothing to be seen of the picture that is to be created. It is the *future* of the person in question. In every human meeting there is not only the past and the immediate happenings of the present to consider. Each man also has within him seeds of the future: a future which lives in all the intentions of his will, though for the present only in seed-form. With every human meeting there arises the challenge of comprehending this element. For this, the formative, living thinking which is able to complete forms as they arise in their process of becoming is not sufficient. There are as yet no finished forms which could be looked upon with understanding. Not even the self-revelatory, spiritual 'hearing' (Inspiration) can help further here, for nothing as yet 'sounds forth' from this source. The individual has here to climb with his own innermost will into the will-intentions of the other person, or, in other words, to receive into his own will the will-intentions of the other. It is a uniting of the higher being in the will. This is an exercise leading towards the stage of Initiation.

These three distinct picture-exercises may also be directed towards man's physical body. First one contemplates everything which is finished and structural in the physical body, principally the nerve-sense organs of the head but also everything which is 'given' structure in the whole body. One should not try, however, to explain everything externally according to natural laws but rather see the whole, the structural form, as a fully painted picture of man's spiritual individuality (Imagination).

The second picture, that which is still in process of arising, is formed if one tries to comprehend all the rhythmical processes of life, in blood, heart and lung (Inspiration).

For the third picture one's attention should be directed towards what is going on in the digestive-movement system of the human organism. Here are to be found the will-intentions which work as seeds of the future. They can be comprehended only through the composing of a picture which is, as it were, not yet begun, whereby one's own, innermost will-intention becomes engaged in the practice of Intuition and unites with the will-intention of the other being.[9]

The question may then be put: who is the painter in these three picture-exercises? It is first and foremost the spiritual individuality of the person whom we are meeting. Without him the three pictures would certainly not be there. In that we are carrying out the three picture-exercises with respect to him, we

generate the three pictures newly within: and the more successful we are in this the more do we unite ourselves with that
spiritual individuality at the stage of Intuition. We become
aware that this individuality is of divine origin. Thus the
meeting between men leads – through the widening and deepening of knowledge – to a profound reverence for the divine
power which awakens in such a meeting. Reverence, devotion –
such is the fundamental attitude on the path which leads to the
knowledge of the spiritual in man and in the world.

Reverence with respect to certain people may in many cases
be well-founded and this is justified so long as it does not lead to
a lack of originality or a slavish dependence. The reverence or
devotion with regard to truth and knowledge referred to here
never makes one dependent.

Reverence & Criticism: exercising positivity in thinking and feeling.

How does the fundamental attitude of reverence relate to man's
critical faculty which is today so strongly formed? This critical
faculty will not allow itself to be done away with. Errors and
weaknesses, all that is untenable and reprehensible should not
be passed over blindly. One should, however, observe what *also*
happens as a result of critical activity: it always creates distance
and also coldness, the person who criticises becomes more
independent. The gulf between subject and object, between
inner and outer, is deepened through each criticism. From this
there springs the task of 'uplifting' criticism through knowledge –
though there is here no implication either of abolition or regret.
Behind everything that is worthy of criticism there is also often
something positive to be observed, and hence criticism becomes a
clarifying element. Thus the substance of justified criticism is
preserved, though united at a higher level with a newly discovered,
stronger, positive content: it is in this sense that the word
'uplifting' is used here. One could clarify the process by
comparing the significance of criticism with that of the shadow

cast by an object in sunlight. The shadows allow the object to stand out even more clearly. But if *only* the shadow is seen, the object itself disappears.

Reverence should not obliterate justified criticism but it can become strong enough to *uplift* any such criticism to a higher stage. The fundamental exercise of *positivity* is an attempt to discover through – or beyond – the negative a new element of positivity.

This exercise of positivity is at present of particular importance on the meditative path, since the one-sided critical tendency has become so great that it isolates man and separates him from the true reality of the world.

How may this positivity be practised? Firstly, it is worth observing one's critical activity and then consciously seeking out what is at any given time also positive in what is being criticised. If one sharpens one's attentiveness and does not allow oneself to be disturbed and diverted from justified criticism, there is always something new and essential that can be found which through criticism had previously remained unnoticed. Concentration upon this positive element is then able to form a capacity of discovering more and more of what is positive in one's surroundings.

The exercise of positivity also creates the necessary soul-foundation for the afore-mentioned 'light-soul-process' between inner and outer.

In the thinking and feeling aspect of the practice of positivity one enters into a fuller connection with the world than one has experienced hitherto. New possibilities for thinking and willing are opened up, and these are always a test of courage. If one has a far-reaching and enlightening experience, one feels 'sure' of oneself; there is nothing new that could make one feel unsettled. But this very attitude harbours an illusion which bars the way to *new* discoveries and *new* deeds. Thus it is good to practise the exercise of open mindedness. This has the same relationship to the original experience as the exercise of positivity has to justified criticism – the experience must likewise be 'up-lifted' for thinking as well as for willing. Insofar as thinking is

concerned this means: however much I may know, there
are always surprising new things to discover and to recognise,
and what is already known can very often mask this newness. Insofar as willing is concerned this means: however much
I may be able to accomplish, there are always new capacities
which I do not as yet possess but which could be realized.
These will very often be veiled precisely through what I
can do already, for one is only too pleased to remain as
one is.

The exercise of positivity described above would go awry if
one were to try to obliterate all criticism and find everything to
be 'good'. In the same way the exercise of open-mindedness
would not be being rightly carried out if the experience were at
this point not taken into account or were even obliterated,
merely in order to be able to remain open-minded. The exercise
demands more. Experience must be raised to a higher stage.
The exercise of open-mindedness strengthens the forces of
courage, for one is venturing forth upon what has not yet been
penetrated or practised: No-one learns how to swim without
entering into the, as yet unknown, realm of water. The power of
the evolving human being, ever growing beyond himself, is
here both tested and strengthened.

At the beginning of the meditative path of knowledge, the
realm of understanding is often regarded as purely theoretical
compared with the 'reality' of 'normal life'. Gradually this
superficial conception changes in a twofold way. The quest for
knowledge becomes more concentrated by degrees and is then
gradually transformed into a process that is decisive for life. At
the same time the sphere of one's own actions is illumined and
opens itself up to self-knowledge. The life-situation in which
one finds oneself, even every ordinary event, gradually begins
to speak a clear language. The picture of one's destiny is drawn
into the quest for knowledge. If this does not happen, the
meditative transformation of one's life is neglected and normal
life dully runs its course beside the quest for knowledge –
which will then always have the tendency to become deadened
into mere theory. Cognition can really only become a living

deed of perception if at the same time one's own destiny is able to shine into one's daily life.

On the meditative path of knowledge, thinking is transformed at every stage. The effort must always be made to allow spiritual facts to become conscious through thought-forms. The mere experience of spiritual facts without penetrating them with one's thoughts leads one to linger in subjectivity rather than to a *science* of the spirit. Only through the medium of thought-forms, whereby spiritual facts become conscious, clear and comprehensible, does one come to spiritual science. But then this is a matter of the reality of the spiritual. Clever thought-formulations may yield a thought-system that is more or less good, but not spiritual science. Spiritual science is spiritual experience which is penetrated through and through by the intellect and which can thereby be shared with other people, even if they have not themselves yet had these experiences.

Chapter Six

Fundamental questions: the significance of the study of spiritual science for the meditative path of knowledge

The study of spiritual science forms a first irreplaceable foundation for the whole meditative path of knowledge. For this path is sufficiently sure only if from the outset it is penetrated by an effective thinking activity. A purely feeling-orientated mode of experience will always have to remain in the realm of uncertainty and unclarity, and will only all too easily slide into superstitious ideas and misunderstandings where what has been unclearly experienced spiritually becomes mixed up with unclear physical sense-experiences. A thorough elaboration in thought of every step is indispensable. And from the first step onwards it is the spiritual facts which become conscious in thinking that further the path of knowledge. Mere thought-formulations without the background of spiritual facts form a severe impediment to the meditative path. Hence in studying it is of particular importance that the thought-content of Spiritual Science is not accepted as true on the authority of the spiritual investigator. For it is precisely such an authority-bound attitude which impedes the direct perception of spiritual facts. It is a matter of not allowing the mental industry of one's studies of Spiritual Science to slacken until one begins to encounter spiritual facts through one's own thought-forms. These appear only through one's own activity, but at the same time objectively, overcoming and overlapping the distinction between subject and object. One's own experience prevails over an external authority. Anthroposophical Spiritual Science contains no dogma, no creed, it is not a system of thoughts or a theory. It is an *'experimental method* in the sphere of the universally human', through which real, spiritual experiences can be had.

Also with regard to the particular exercises of the meditative path of knowledge, thorough study is necessary beforehand. If one wishes to carry out an exercise, this can only happen rightly and consciously if the context in which it stands is clear and if, in addition, another complementary exercise through which alone a harmonious balance can be established comes eventually to form part of the original exercise. In the preface to the third edition of his book, *Knowledge of the higher worlds: how is it achieved?* (GA10), Rudolf Steiner emphasizes this: 'Intimate penetration into the text is necessary; it ought to be a stipulation that one particular matter shall not be grasped only through what is said about it specifically but through much that is said about quite other things. In this way it will be realised that the core of the matter does not lie in *one* truth, but in the harmony of them all. This must be very earnestly borne in mind by those who wish to carry out the exercises. A particular exercise can be correctly understood and also correctly carried out; yet it can have a wrong effect if someone who is practising it does not add to it another exercise which resolves the one-sidedness of the first into a harmony in the soul' (translation of sixth English Edition, 1969).

Every meditation is only possible through an individual, free initiative. A meditation can never be introduced into a person from without if it is to represent a step on the path of knowledge along the lines as have been characterised here. It would then be something altogether different and would have to have a different name. Nor can outer rules determine how much a particular person should meditate. Everything on this meditative path of knowledge must arise in an individual, and hence always different, way in accordance with the possibilities of the individual life-situation, constitution and social relationships. This is, however, something which can only be judged and determined by each individual himself. A description of the meditative path of knowledge is an account of experiences and possibilities which have been tried out: it should never be understood as a prescription by which one should be bound. The source of such experiences resides in the power of the individual himself. The meditation is always an activity that represents an excess over anything that one might otherwise 'expect', still less 'demand', from anyone. Hence in the course of a meditative path of knowledge there is also always an element of individual motivation involved, and this too will have a different colouring and content with every person. Only through conscious, individual motivation will a meditation be able to have the effective power that is proper to it. If one were to meditate simply to try it out or out of sheer curiosity, no lasting effects would result.

There are inner as well as outer hindrances which can make progress on the meditative path of knowledge impossible. The inner hindrances are overcome through the meditations, which lead to new stages of consciousness. The outer hindrances are overcome through the basic exercises, if these are forged into fundamental attitudes of life as have been here characterised:

1. Control of thoughts (see p.9)
2. Control of will (see p.34)
3. Calmness, composure in feeling (see p.37)
4. Positivity, thinking and feeling (see p.44)
5. Open-mindedness, thinking in connection with willing (see p.45)

The first three exercises form a triad in thinking, willing and feeling. Positivity unfolds itself in thinking and feeling and leads to an open relationship with one's surroundings. Open-mindedness confers upon thinking in association with willing a certain maturity and leads to a glimpse into future experiences.

These five basic forces or qualities are then gathered together in a sixth exercise, where one cultivates all five modes of conduct equally and regularly in order that a whole organism of these human forces of development can mature in a harmonious way. These fundamental exercises are frequently called 'subsidiary exercises'. This term, however, does not mean 'exercises of a lower rank' but, rather, exercises which form a necessary, harmonious foundation in life *beside* the other meditative exercises, which overcome the inner hindrances through an evolution of consciousness and an awakening of the forces sleeping in man. They prove to be the sure foundation for the meditative path of knowledge, the ground upon which alone the other, 'consciousness-awakening', exercises may rightly be carried out.

Notes

1. See *Guidance in Esoteric Training* Rudolf Steiner Press, London 1972) p.14.
2. A description of this exercise in a wider connection may be found in Rudolf Steiner's lecture *Das Anschauungserlebnis der Denktätigkeit und der Sprachtätigkeit*, Dornach 20 April 1923 in *Was wollte das Goetheanum und was soll die Anthroposophie* (GA 84)
3. Rudolf Steiner: *Knowledge of the Higher Worlds: how is it achieved?* (quotations from 6th English Edition, R.S.P. 1969), the chapter entitled, *R. Steiner, The Stages of initiation, 1. Preparation.*
4. *Knowledge of the Higher Worlds: how is it achieved?*
5. Compare with the description in Rudolf Steiner's lecture of 28th of March 1910 in the cycle, *Macrocosm and Microcosm* R.S.P. London 1968.
6. See Rudolf Steiner's lecture on *Occult Science and Occult Development*, 1 May 1913 (in the volume of that title, R.S.P. 1966).
7. Compare Rudolf Steiner, lecture of 30 November 1919 in *The Mission of the Archangel Michael* (Anthroposophic Press New York 1980)
8. Compare Rudolf Steiner, *Man: Positive and Negative*, lecture of 10 March 1910, in *Paths of Experience*, Rudolf Steiner Publicity Company London 1934.
9. Compare Rudolf Steiner's description in a letter to the Members of the Anthroposophical Society of 18 May 1924 on 'The Pictorial Nature of Man', *The Life, Nature and Cultivation of Anthroposophy*, Anthroposophical Society in Great Britain 1975.

Other Books from Hawthorn Press

Eye of the Needle
His Life and Working encounter with Anthroposophy
Bernard Lievegoed
An exploration of Lievegoed's personal life, and his wide-ranging interests.
112 pp; 216 x 138mm; 1 869 890 50 7; pb.

In Place of the Self
How Drugs Work
Ron Dunselman
Why are heroin, alcohol, hashish, ecstasy, LSD and tobacco attractive substances for so many people? Why are unusual, visionary and 'high' experiences so important to users? These and other questions about drugs and drug use are answered comprehensively in this book.
304 pp; 216 x 138mm; 1 869 890 72 8; hb.

Lighting Fires
Deepening Education through Meditation
Jorgen Smit
The author addresses the inner path of the human 'becoming' who lives in every adult and child. Often, the teachers who 'light fires rather than fill buckets' work on deepening their teaching through meditation and personal development.
96 pp; 216 x 138mm; 1 869 890 45 0; pb.

Life Patterns
Responding to Life's Questions, Crises and Challenges
Jerry Schöttelndreier
Translated by Jakob Cornelis
Life Patterns offers a method that enables individuals to take stock of their present life situation, to understand their roots, to gain practical and spiritual insights into their own personal setting and to consider the way ahead.
64pp; 216 x 138mm; 1 869 890 27 2; pb.

More Precious than Light
How Dialogue can Transform Relationships and Build Community
Margreet van den Brink

Profound changes are taking place as people awaken to the experience of the Christ in themselves, and in significant human encounter. As tradition fades, individual and social paths of growth emerge. These are helped by building relationships through helping conversations, through dialogue, through exploring heartfelt questions which can lead to liberating personal insights.

'The true community spirit values differences as well as harmony, is open rather than closed. Challenge, support, questioning and empathy are all needed. Knowing when one or the other is appropriate depends on presence of mind. It depends as much on intuition as on a knowledge of group work.'

160 pp; 216 x 138mm; 1 869 890 83 3; pb.

Personal and Social Transformation
Freedom, Equality and Fraternity in Everyday Life
Jörgen Smit

Translated by Simon Blaxand de Lange

Throughout history revolutions have challenged people to transform society on the basis of freedom, equality and fraternity. Attempts are still being made to find a path beyond communism and liberal capitalism. Jorgen Smit, a lecturer on Steiner education, argues that individuals can and must take the responsibility for developing real freedom in everyday life and must learn how to translate the rhetoric of equality into reality.

96pp; 216 x 138mm; 1 869 890 39 6; pb;

Renewing Education
Selected Writings on Steiner Education
Francis Edmunds

This collection of essays is concerned with the spiritual basis of an individual's development from childhood onwards and will be a valuable reference work for all teachers. Francis Edmunds has travelled widely and his talks and writings, emphasising the responsibility of adults and educators towards children, have inspired and educated a world-wide audience.

136pp; 216 x 138mm; 1 869 890 31 0; pb.

Rudolf Steiner on Education
A Compendium
Roy Wilkinson
Here is an accessible introduction to the educational philosophy of Rudolf Steiner—the pioneer of a comprehensive, co-educational form of education for children from kindergarten to the end of high school.
168 pp; 216 x 138mm; 1 869 890 51 5; pb.

Rudolf Steiner
An Introduction
Rudi Lissau
This portrait of Steiner's life and work aims to point out the relevance of his activities to contemporary social and human concerns.
192 pp; 210 x 135mm; 1 869 890 06 8; pb.

Seven Soul Types
Max Stibbe
A description of the seven soul types of man, indicating the most significant inner and outer characteristics of each. Recognition of soul types can be invaluable in communicating with others in social, educational or therapeutic situations.
128 pp; 216 x 138mm; 1 869 890 44 2; pb.

Soulways
Development, Crises and Illnesses of the Soul
Rudolf Treichler
Soulways offers insights into personal growth through the phases and turning points of human life. A profound picture of child and adult development is given, including the developmental needs, potentials and questions of each stage. Drawing on his work as a psychiatrist, Treichler also explores the developmental disorders of soul life—addictions, neuroses, hysteria, anorexia and schizophrenia.
320pp; 210 x 135mm; 1 869 890 13 2; pb.

Tapestries
Weaving Life's Journey
Betty Staley

Tapestries gives a moving and wise guide to women's life phases. Drawing on original biographies of a wide variety of women, informed by personal experience and by her understanding of anthroposophy, Betty Staley offers a vivid account of life journeys. This book helps readers reflect on their own lives and prepare for the next step in weaving their own biographical tapestry.
336pp; 216 x 138mm; 1 869 890 15 9; pb.

Thresholds
Near Life Experiences
Gabriel Bradford Millar

People returning to life from serious accidents sometimes describe their near-death experiences. This book gathers together accounts and revelations experienced in the midst of everyday life.
192 pp; 216 x 138mm; photographs; 1 869 890 68 X; pb.

The Twelve Senses
Albert Soesman

The author provides a lively look at the senses—not merely the normal five senses, but twelve: touch, life, self-movement, balance, smell, taste, vision, temperature, hearing, language, the conceptual and the ego senses.
176 pp; 210 x 135mm; 1 869 890 22 1; pb.

Workways: Seven Stars to steer by
Biography Workbook for Building a more Enterprising Life
Kees Locher and Jos van der Brug

This biography workbook helps you consider your working life, and make more conscious choices, at a time of great change in our 'workways'. Background readings, thirty seven exercises and creative activities are carefully structured for individuals or self-help groups.
352pp; 297 x 210mm; 1 869 890 89 2; pb.

Orders

If you have difficulties ordering from a bookshop, you can order direct from:

Scottish Book Source, 137 Dundee Street, Edinburgh, EH11 1BG
Tel. 0131 229 6800 Fax. 0131 229 9070